Wind Power

by C. A. Barnhart

PEARSON
Scott Foresman

What You Already Know

People, animals, and plants all need natural resources to live. Some natural resources are replaced all the time. Although renewable natural resources are in abundant supply, they must be well cared for. Soil is one important renewable resource. Soil is renewed through weathering, erosion, and deposition. Soil contains humus. Humus is made from decaying plant and animal matter. Clay, silt, and sand are different sized particles of rock in soil. Good farming can replace nutrients in soil. Many things can be made from soil.

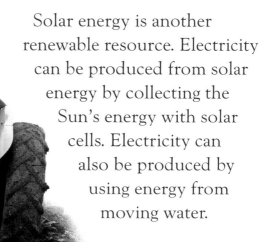

Solar energy is another renewable resource. Electricity can be produced from solar energy by collecting the Sun's energy with solar cells. Electricity can also be produced by using energy from moving water.

Plowing the remains of plants into the field returns nutrients to the soil.

Other resources that we rely upon, including fossil fuels such as natural gas, coal, and petroleum, are not easily or quickly replaced. An ore is a mineral-rich rock found in Earth's crust. Many nonrenewable mineral resources are found in ores. All natural resources are important and must be used

wind farm

wisely. Production of energy is a major use of fossil fuel. Electricity and gasoline keep our factories operating, our houses warm, and our transportation moving.

There are several ways to practice conservation of our natural resources. One way is by recycling. Recycling reduces the amount of nonrenewable resources we use. Some paper and plastics are recyclable. Another way is to increase the use of renewable resources to produce power.

Wind is another natural source of renewable energy. People have used the power of the wind for centuries. Today, we are using it more and more. Read on to find out about wind power.

The Power of Wind

In order to learn how wind can be used as a source of power, first you must understand what wind is. Wind is caused by differences in temperature in Earth's atmosphere. Air flows constantly over Earth. Pockets of air rise from Earth's surface as they become warmer and their molecules become less dense. Cool air, which has more densely packed molecules, rushes in to take the place of the warm air. This movement of cold, heavy air falling and warm, lighter air rising is called wind.

Wind can have a powerful effect on landforms, or features of Earth's surface. Wind can cause erosion, changing the shape of rock formations.

Blowing wind changes the shapes of rocks by erosion.

A toy pinwheel demonstrates how wind power turns a wheel.

Global Winds

easterlies

westerlies

trade winds

doldrums

trade winds

westerlies

easterlies

Easterlies are winds that blow from east to west. Westerlies are winds that blow from west to east. Trade winds are found above and below the equator and blow almost constantly. Few winds blow in the doldrums.

Earth's prevailing winds form at the equator where the air is hot and rises high into the atmosphere. Little wind results. On each side of the equator, however, a band of brisk winds blows toward it. These winds are drawn toward the equator by the heated air moving upward. Winds farther north and farther south are also affected by the hot air from the equator when they meet cold air from the North and South Poles.

Although you can't see wind, it is a very powerful force. The spinning motion of this toy pinwheel is physical evidence of the wind's effect.

Wind for Movement

Until the 1900s, the main power for ships was the wind. Today, sailing ships are used mostly for education and sport.

A sailboat of today is not very different from ships of ancient times. All are moved by the wind. All have sails controlled by ropes.

A newer and more portable sailboat is the sailboard. It is a surfboard with a sail. The rider sails or windsurfs while standing up and steers by pulling in and letting out the sail. Sailboards tip easily.

Sailboats and sailboards used for sport have triangular sails to catch the wind.

The ancient Egyptians were the first people known to use the wind to move boats. They are credited with developing cloth sails around 3300 B.C. The first sails were square. Square sails worked well when the wind came from behind the boat. The wind would then fill the sail and move the boat forward. If the wind came from the wrong direction, however, the only way to move a boat with a square sail was by rowing.

Clipper ships have many sails that can catch the wind.

About two thousand years ago, ships traveling on the Mediterranean Sea began using triangular sails. The sail was fixed to a pole called a mast. Ropes were used to move the sail from one side to another. The sail could catch the wind from any direction. Later, ships were rigged with a combination of square and triangular sails. Many sails meant more power and speed from the wind. Ships could be larger. A clipper ship is an example of a ship with such rigging.

glider

Gliders, hang gliders, and balloons move through the air and return to Earth's surface using only wind power. Gliders fly along wind currents after being towed into the air by a plane or after catching the wind on a hillside or cliff. Hang gliders catch the wind in the same way. Weather balloons are carried by winds to make weather observations. A kite catches the wind in its sails and soars through the air. All these ways of flying use the wind not only to go higher, farther, and faster, but also to steer and to land.

A kite is released into the air. You can guide it with a string while the wind carries it.

Wind for Machines

People have used wind power to operate machines for centuries. Wind is turned into power for machines in a way similar to the way a paper pinwheel works. A wheel catches the wind and turns, changing the power of the wind into a power that works machinery.

In the United States, windmills were used on farms to pump water from wells deep underground. These windmills had a wheel that could turn in any direction to face the wind. The wheel was guided by a vane at the other end of a horizontal pole. This horizontal pole transferred power to a vertical pole. This power operated a pump underground.

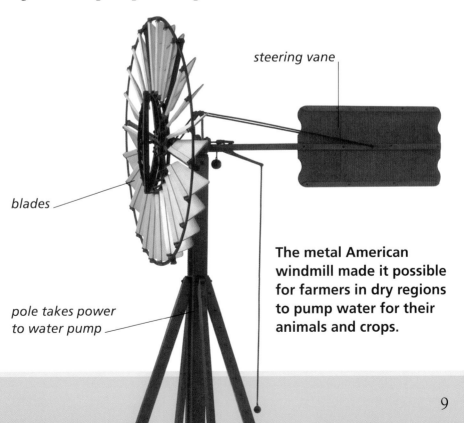

steering vane

blades

pole takes power
to water pump

The metal American windmill made it possible for farmers in dry regions to pump water for their animals and crops.

The earliest known windmills were built in what is now Iran, about fourteen hundred years ago. These early windmills had a wheel with sails that turned as they caught the wind. The wheel was fastened to the top of a pole. The wheel turned this pole. These early windmills were used to grind grain and pump water.

By about 1100, windmills appeared in Europe, especially in what is now the Netherlands. There they were used mostly to pump water away from land that was often flooded by the sea. In these Dutch windmills, the wheel or sails were attached to a horizontal pole. People used gears and pulleys to transfer the power from the horizontal pole to a vertical pole.

Windmills

A windmill such as this was used to grind grain. This model shows the gearwheel, which changed the direction of power from horizontal to vertical. The grindstone was used for grinding the grain.

gearwheel

grindstone

This vertical pole worked the pump that was located at the bottom of the windmill. Later windmills had wheels that could be turned in any direction to face the wind. This marked a great improvement in their efficiency. These new windmills could use the wind no matter which way it was blowing.

These windmills in La Mancha, Spain, were used for grinding grain.

Wind for Electricity

Most electricity in the United States is produced in power plants that burn fossil fuels or use nuclear power or water power. There is a limited supply of fossil fuels. When fossil fuels are burned, pollutants are released into the environment. Nuclear waste from nuclear power plants is difficult and expensive to dispose of.

One solution to these problems is to produce electricity by using the wind. It is an abundant, renewable resource, which makes it an appealing source of power. Wind is also appealing because it doesn't cause pollution.

Electricity produced by wind is generated in a wind turbine. This is a kind of modern windmill designed especially to make electricity. The wind turbine has three huge blades at the top of a tall tower. These blades are turned by the wind. Similar to the Dutch and American windmills, the blades are attached to a horizontal pole. The pole turns a wheel directly behind the blades. The turbine generates electricity that is then sent over power wires. Groups of wind turbines built in one place are called wind farms.

A wind farm such as this one contains many wind turbines.

Fossil Fuels

Smoke rising from a power plant that burns fossil fuels spreads through the air and pollutes the environment.

The turbines that generate electricity are designed to increase the amount of power made by the rotating blades. By increasing their power, turbines are able to produce greater amounts of electricity.

A wind farm must be located where there are steady winds. Some wind farms can produce enough electricity for a small town. Some farmers have put up a few wind turbines to produce just enough electricity to meet their own needs. Some large electric companies have begun to build very large wind farms.

Another location for wind farms is in the ocean, along a coastline. The winds are steadier over the water. They can produce electricity more efficiently.

Offshore wind farms are built in coastal waters, where they take advantage of steady winds.

Some people object to wind turbines claiming they are noisy. However, most of the turbines are no noisier than leaves rustling in a breeze. Another reason people may object is that they feel that wind turbines are not very nice-looking. But perhaps the benefits of using them, such as less air pollution, will make them seem more attractive.

All countries of the world need more electricity. At the same time, pollution is becoming more of a problem. Use of the world's winds to generate electricity makes wind farms an increasingly appealing way to get the electricity we need without harming the environment.

Glossary

efficiency   production of something with
                          little waste of time or effort

gearwheel   a wheel with grooves that fit
                          into another gear

power plants   stations that generate power,
                          often by burning fossil fuels

prevailing winds   winds that are most common,
                          especially in terms of reliability,
                          force, or direction

rig   to fit a boat or ship with equipment,
                          such as a sail, mast, and ropes

turbine   a machine that has a rotating wheel
                          with paddles attached to it that spin
                          as the wheel turns

wind farm   a cluster of wind turbines built near
                          each other to generate electricity